FRANCIS FRITH'S
DERBYSHIRE
REVISITED

PHOTOGRAPHIC MEMORIES

Roly Smith, president of the Outdoor Writers' Guild and member of the British Guild of Travel Writers, is a freelance writer and editor, and the author of over 30 books on walking and the countryside. Based in Bakewell in the Peak District, Roly took voluntary early retirement from his position as Head of Information Services with the Peak District National Park in May 1997, to concentrate on his freelance career. Previously he enjoyed a 20-year, award-winning career in daily paper journalism, latterly on the *Birmingham Post* and *Evening Mail*. He is vice president of the South Yorkshire and North East Derbyshire area of the Ramblers' Association.

FRANCIS FRITH'S
PHOTOGRAPHIC MEMORIES

DERBYSHIRE
REVISITED

PHOTOGRAPHIC MEMORIES

ROLY SMITH

First published in the United Kingdom in 2005 by
Frith Book Company Ltd

Hardback Edition 2005
ISBN 1-85937-460-3

British Library Cataloguing in Publication Data

Francis Frith's Derbyshire Revisited -
Photographic Memories
Roly Smith
Frith Book Company Ltd

Frith's Barn, Teffont,
Salisbury, Wiltshire SP3 5QP
Tel: +44 (0) 1722 716 376
Email: info@francisfrith.co.uk
www.francisfrith.co.uk

Printed and bound in Great Britain

Front Cover: **GOYT VALLEY,** *The Stepping Stones 1914* 67587
Frontispiece: **BAKEWELL,** *The Bridge 1923* 73884

The colour-tinting is for illustrative purposes only, and is not intended to be historically accurate

AS WITH ANY HISTORICAL DATABASE THE FRITH ARCHIVE IS CONSTANTLY
BEING CORRECTED AND IMPROVED AND THE PUBLISHERS WOULD
WELCOME INFORMATION ON OMISSIONS OR INACCURACIES

CONTENTS

FRANCIS FRITH
VICTORIAN PIONEER

FRANCIS FRITH, founder of the world-famous photographic archive, was a complex and multi-talented man. A devout Quaker and a highly successful Victorian businessman, he was philosophical by nature and pioneering in outlook.

By 1855 he had already established a wholesale grocery business in Liverpool, and sold it for the astonishing sum of £200,000, which is the equivalent today of over £15,000,000. Now a very rich man, he was able to indulge his passion for travel. As a child he had pored over travel books written by early explorers, and his fancy and imagination had been stirred by family holidays to the sublime mountain regions of Wales and Scotland. 'What lands of spirit-stirring and enriching scenes and places!' he had written. He was to return to these scenes of grandeur in later years to 'recapture the thousands of vivid and tender memories', but with a different purpose. Now in his thirties, and captivated by the new science of photography, Frith set out on a series of pioneering journeys up the Nile and to the

Near East that occupied him from 1856 until 1860.

INTRIGUE AND EXPLORATION

These far-flung journeys were packed with intrigue and adventure. In his life story, written when he was sixty-three, Frith tells of being held captive by bandits, and of fighting 'an awful midnight battle to the very point of surrender with a deadly pack of hungry, wild dogs'. Wearing flowing Arab costume, Frith arrived at Akaba by camel sixty years before Lawrence of Arabia, where he encountered 'desert princes and rival sheikhs, blazing with jewel-hilted swords'.

He was the first photographer to venture beyond the sixth cataract of the Nile. Africa was still the mysterious 'Dark Continent', and Stanley and Livingstone's historic meeting was a decade into the future. The conditions for picture taking confound belief. He laboured for hours in his wicker dark-room in the sweltering heat of the desert, while the volatile chemicals fizzed dangerously in their trays. Back in London he exhibited his photographs and was 'rapturously cheered' by members of the Royal Society. His reputation as a photographer was made overnight.

VENTURE OF A LIFE-TIME

Characteristically, Frith quickly spotted the opportunity to create a new business as a specialist publisher of photographs. He lived in an era of immense and sometimes violent change.

For the poor in the early part of Victoria's reign work was exhausting and the hours long, and people had precious little free time to enjoy themselves. Most had no transport other than a cart or gig at their disposal, and rarely travelled far beyond the boundaries of their own town or village. However, by the 1870s the railways had threaded their way across the country, and Bank Holidays and half-day Saturdays had been made obligatory by Act of Parliament. All of a sudden the working man and his family were able to enjoy days out and see a little more of the world.

With typical business acumen, Francis Frith foresaw that these new tourists would enjoy having souvenirs to commemorate their days out. In 1860 he married Mary Ann Rosling and set out on a new career: his aim was to photograph every city, town and village in Britain. For the next thirty years he travelled the country by train and by pony and trap, producing fine photographs of seaside resorts and beauty spots that were keenly bought by millions of Victorians. These prints were painstakingly pasted into family albums and pored over during the dark nights of winter, rekindling precious memories of summer excursions.

THE RISE OF FRITH & CO

Frith's studio was soon supplying retail shops all over the country. To meet the demand he gathered about him a small team of photographers, and published the work of independent artist-photographers of the calibre of Roger Fenton and Francis Bedford. In order to gain some understanding of the scale of Frith's business one only has to look at the catalogue issued by Frith & Co in 1886: it runs to some 670 pages, listing not only many thousands of views of the British Isles but also many photographs of most European countries, and China, Japan, the USA and Canada - note the sample page shown here from the hand-written Frith & Co ledgers recording the pictures. By 1890 Frith had created the greatest specialist photographic publishing company in the world, with over 2,000 sales outlets - more than the combined number that Boots and WH Smith have today! The picture on the next page shows the Frith & Co display board at Ingleton in the Yorkshire Dales (left of window). Beautifully constructed with a mahogany frame and gilt inserts, it could display up to a dozen local scenes.

POSTCARD BONANZA

The ever-popular holiday postcard we know today took many years to develop. In 1870 the Post Office issued the first plain cards, with a pre-printed stamp on one face. In 1894 they allowed other publishers' cards to be sent through the mail with an attached adhesive halfpenny stamp. Demand grew rapidly, and in 1895 a new size of postcard was permitted called the court card, but there was little room for illustration. In 1899, a year after Frith's death, a new card measuring 5.5 x 3.5 inches became the standard format, but it was not until 1902 that the divided back came into being, so that the address and message could be on one face and a full-size illustration on the other. Frith & Co were in the vanguard of postcard development: Frith's sons Eustace and Cyril continued their father's monumental task, expanding the number of views offered to the public and recording more and more places in

Britain, as the coasts and countryside were opened up to mass travel.

Francis Frith had died in 1898 at his villa in Cannes, his great project still growing. The archive he created continued in business for another seventy years. By 1970 it contained over a third of a million pictures showing 7,000 British towns and villages.

FRANCIS FRITH'S LEGACY

Frith's legacy to us today is of immense significance and value, for the magnificent archive of evocative photographs he created provides a unique record of change in the cities, towns and villages throughout Britain over a century and more. Frith and his fellow studio photographers revisited locations many times down the years to update their views, compiling for us an enthralling and colourful pageant of British life and character.

We are fortunate that Frith was dedicated to recording the minutiae of everyday life. For it is this sheer wealth of visual data, the painstaking chronicle of changes in dress, transport, street layouts, buildings, housing, engineering and landscape that captivates us so much today. His remarkable images offer us a powerful link with the past and with the lives of our ancestors.

THE VALUE OF THE ARCHIVE TODAY

Computers have now made it possible for Frith's many thousands of images to be accessed almost instantly. Frith's images are increasingly used as visual resources, by social historians, by researchers into genealogy and ancestry, by architects and town planners, and by teachers involved in local history projects.

In addition, the archive offers every one of us an opportunity to examine the places where we and our families have lived and worked down the years. Highly successful in Frith's own era, the archive is now, a century and more on, entering a new phase of popularity. Historians consider the Francis Frith Collection to be of prime national importance. It is the only archive of its kind remaining in private ownership. Francis Frith's archive is now housed in an historic timber barn in the beautiful village of Teffont in Wiltshire. Its founder would not recognize the archive office as it is today. In place of the many thousands of dusty boxes containing glass plate negatives and an all-pervading odour of photographic chemicals, there are now ranks of computer screens. He would be amazed to watch his images travelling round the world at unimaginable speeds through internet lines.

The archive's future is both bright and exciting. Francis Frith, with his unshakeable belief in making photographs available to the greatest number of people, would undoubtedly approve of what is being done today with his lifetime's work. His photographs depicting our shared past are now bringing pleasure and enlightenment to millions around the world a century and more after his death.

DERBYSHIRE
REVISITED
AN INTRODUCTION

DERBYSHIRE stands at the crossroads of Britain, on the border between the highlands and the lowlands, and it can be said to enjoy the best of both worlds. The scenic contrasts of the county range from the rugged Pennine moorlands of the Dark Peak to the pastoral lowland meadows of the Lower Dove and Trent. This position at the crossroads of Britain is reflected in the effect that man has had on the landscape. Towns and villages in the Peak District are often small and isolated; they are built not of the red brick of the lowlands, but of the native stone. Here also there are many more stone-built reminders of the ancient past. These include the many burial mounds or 'lows' which crown so many hills in the Peak District, and prehistoric monuments such as the Arbor Low stone circle near Parsley Hay. Once we have crossed the north-south border, north of Ashbourne, the hedgerows and arable fields which typify the Midlands give way to mile after mile of drystone walls criss-crossing stony pastures, where pastoral farming of sheep and cattle predominates.

In terms of geology, Derbyshire is divided into four distinct regions, which in turn have shaped its landscape and its towns and villages. These are the southern clay and sandstone area, roughly south of a line from Derby to Ashbourne; the sandy coal measures east of Derby and Chesterfield with the band of Magnesian limestone around Bolsover and Whitwell; the central limestone plateau of the White Peak between Ashbourne and Castleton; and the high millstone grit moorlands in the north of the county, which are usually known as the Dark Peak.

The largely Carboniferous rocks of the northern half of the county were laid down in

GOYT VALLEY, *The Stepping Stones 1914* 67587

semi-tropical conditions around 350 million years ago, when what was to become Derbyshire was several degrees south of the Equator and flooded by a warm, shallow sea. This was when the enormously thick beds of limestone (which are now exposed as the White Peak plateau) were laid down as millions of tiny sea creatures died and drifted down to the sea bed. Following a series of minor volcanic events, the limestone was covered by beds of coarse grit and silt brought down by rivers flowing from the north. This was compressed and compacted to form alternating layers of millstone grit and softer shales; these now form the moorland areas known as the Dark Peak and the broad shale valleys below, now occupied by Derbyshire's major rivers such as the Derwent and Wye.

The whole 'sandwich' was overlaid yet again by the coal-bearing tropical rain forests of the Carboniferous period, which created the coal measures of the former Derbyshire-Nottinghamshire coalfield, running from Chesterfield south to Ilkeston. At the end of the Carboniferous period, these sedimentary rocks were subjected to enormously strong folding and faulting, followed by an uplift in the earth's crust which created the famous Derbyshire Dome anticline. The action of glaciers and the frost-thaw conditions of successive Ice Ages wore down the dome from the centre, creating the now-familiar up-turned horseshoe of gritstone and shale with the coal measures on either side, and the older limestone exposed in the middle.

The red-coloured sandstones and clays of the south of the county were laid down after the Carboniferous rocks to the north in the arid, semi-desert conditions of the Triassic period, up to 280 million years ago. These rocks are much softer and more susceptible to erosion; they have created the richer and more fertile soils of the south, over which the Trent, Dove and Derwent have deposited their alluvium.

It is not surprising that the varied geology of the county has played a major part in the building materials and styles of the vernacular architecture of its towns and villages.

The first evidence of man in Derbyshire is found on the bleak, inhospitable moors of the Dark Peak. Tiny slivers of flint - known as microliths - have been found in the sides of the groughs or haggs which dissect the moorland; these microliths had been hafted on to arrows which were discarded by Mesolithic (Middle Stone Age) hunters, perhaps 10,000 years ago. Few remains of the temporary camps of these first hunter-gatherers have survived, but most of the great prehistoric monuments of Derbyshire are to be found in the uplands of the Peak District. Chief among these is the isolated prostrate stone circle and henge at Arbor Low, high on the White Peak plateau near Parsley Hay, which is sometimes dubbed 'the Stonehenge of the North'.

There are estimated to be at least 500 barrows - or burial mounds - scattered across the county, mostly dating from the Bronze Age. Nearly all are situated on hilltops or high points in the landscape, and paradoxically most have the suffix 'low' (the word derives from the Old English 'hlaw', meaning 'burial mound' or 'hill'). The Iron Age (about 2,000 years ago) was the age of the hill fort, and impressive examples can be found at places like Mam Tor at the head of the Hope Valley and Fin Cop, overlooking Monsal Dale.

It was the abundant and easily accessible lead ore found in the limestone areas of the White Peak which first attracted the Romans into Derbyshire in the latter part of the 1st century. Forts were built at Navio, near Brough in the Hope Valley, and at Melandra, near Glossop at the entrance to Longdendale. Later, more substantial settlements were made around the warm springs at Buxton (Aquae Arnemetia) and on the outskirts of modern Derby, where the fort of Little Chester (Derventio) has been excavated.

The period between the Romans and the Normans - usually termed 'the Dark Ages' - saw a wonderful flowering of art and sculpture, witnessed by Derbyshire's outstanding collection of Saxon preaching crosses. Excellent examples can be found at Bakewell, Bradbourne, Eyam, Hope and Ilam in the Peak District, while Repton's surviving Saxon crypt and chancel bear evidence to this sleepy little town's former importance as a famous Mercian monastery and the burial place of the Saxon St Wystan.

The first Anglian people who colonised the Peak District were known as the Pecsaete, or people of the Peak, while the south of the county fell under the influence of that powerful kingdom of Middle England - Mercia. For a period, Derbyshire appears to have acted as a buffer between the states of Mercia and Northumbria before Mercia finally attained ascendancy by the end of the 8th century. It was during this time that Derby first got its name: it derives from an Old Scandinavian word meaning 'the place where deer are seen'. It later reverted back to its Saxon name, Northworthy, and then returned to the Danish name, Derby, in the 10th century.

By the time of the Norman Conquest, much of the present-day pattern of villages and towns in Derbyshire was well-established, as we can see from the Domesday Book of 1086. Only seven churches - at Ashbourne, Bakewell, Bradbourne, Darley, Hope, Repton and Wirksworth - are mentioned as being in existence before the Conquest, and some still show signs of Saxon work today, particularly those at Bradbourne and Repton. Much of the Derbyshire part of the Peak District was held by the king at the time of Domesday; it was part of the Royal Forest of the Peak - a 40-square-mile hunting ground preserved for royalty. Along with the lead mines, the Forest was administered from Peveril Castle at Castleton; the castle was built by William Peverel, one of the Conquerer's illegitimate sons, who also built the original stronghold at Haddon Hall, near Bakewell. Later Norman castles and fortified manors were built at Codnor, South Wingfield, Hardwick, and Haddon, and there are fine Norman churches at Melbourne, Steetley, and Ault Hucknall, and traces of Norman work in the churches at Bakewell and Barlborough, among many others.

During the Middle Ages, the wealth of Derbyshire was founded on its lead and wool, and some of the fine churches, such as the beautiful, Perpendicular-towered 'Cathedral of the Peak' at Tideswell and All Saints at Youlgreave, are founded upon those riches. The Middle Ages also saw the growth of the large estates. The great Derbyshire families (such as the Cavendishes, Dukes of Devonshire, at Bolsover, Chatsworth, and Hardwick; the Vernons, Dukes of Rutland, at Haddon and Sudbury; the Stanhopes at Elvaston; the Harpur-Crewes at Calke; and the Curzons at Kedleston) grew rich on these estates and their produce, building the county's wonderful heritage of stately homes and parklands.

This was also the time of the first enclosures of the large medieval open fields from the moorland, which still covered much of the upland part of the county. These large, irregular fields on the outskirts of villages contrast strongly with the narrow linear fields leading from the village crofts, which were the villagers' own strip fields. The pattern of medieval enclosure is well shown in White Peak villages such as Chelmorton and Castleton, where it has been 'fossilised' by the drystone walls.

The linear bumps and hollows on the limestone plateau are evidence of the work of 't'owd man' - the local name for former generations of lead miners. Lead mining was an important industry in the White Peak for well over 1,000 years, starting with the Romans and ending in the 19th century when cheaper imports became available. There are estimated to be about 30,000 abandoned workings in the area. The best preserved of these is the Magpie Mine, near Sheldon, which was worked more or less continuously for 200 years. Peak District lead miners were also usually farmers as well, and this dual economy existed in the area as the mainstay of the local economy for centuries, bequeathing a rich legacy in the language and landscape.

It was the power of the Derbyshire rivers - particularly the Derwent - which attracted the first real industrialists to the county. Foremost among these were John Lombe and George Sorocold, who established Derby's Silk Mill in 1718, and Richard Arkwright, who built the first successful water-powered cotton mill at Cromford in 1771. Arkwright also built the first 'model village' for his workers nearby, and other cotton mills at Cressbrook, Bakewell and else-where. Cromford could well be described as one of the birthplaces of the Industrial Revolution; here Arkwright first pioneered the idea of mass production. Downstream, Jedediah Strutt's cotton mill at Belper was founded a few years later in 1776, and he later developed a calico and tape mill in Derby.

The presence of relatively easily obtainable supplies of coal from the North Derbyshire, the Leicestershire and South Derbyshire, and the Yorkshire, Nottinghamshire and Derbyshire coalfields, all on the east of the county, made Derbyshire one of the biggest sources of power in the late 19th and early 20th centuries. By 1910, there were estimated to be over 175 coal mines in Derbyshire, employing 52,000 people. Output was more than 16.5 million tons in 1906, and the proximity of ironstone and limestone placed the county in an ideal position for iron and steel production.

The building of the Derby Canal by Benjamin Outram in 1796 proved to be a key element in turning a prosperous market town into a leading centre of industry. The famous Derby porcelain factory had been established by William Duesbury around 1750, and helped by local supplies of coal, an iron-founding industry followed. The same Benjamin Outram had, with Francis Beresford, founded the famous Butterley Iron Works in 1790, and was joint promoter, with Richard Arkwright, of the Cromford Canal, which was designed to link Arkwright's mills at Cromford to the River Trent and the Midlands.

Railways followed, including George Stephenson's Derby to Leeds line through the Derwent Valley. By 1840, no less than three railway companies were operating lines to Derby from Nottingham, Leeds and Birmingham respectively. Within five years they had amalgamated to form the Midland Railway, and benefiting from its central position on the east coast line, Derby became a major railway centre and terminus. The Midland Railway established its locomotive and carriage works there soon after its formation, and more foundries soon followed in the town to provide other components for the burgeoning railways. The construction of the Midland Line followed in 1863, providing the lucrative link between London and Manchester through the Wye Valley and the hills of the Peak District. Industrial towns like Derby and Chesterfield expanded rapidly during the 19th century, and by the time that Derby was awarded city status a hundred years later in 1977, it had become one of the major industrial and engineering centres of the Midlands.

But in the smaller towns and villages of Derbyshire, a distinctive vernacular architecture had developed, usually based on the underlying geology of the area. Thus in the limestone area of the White Peak, cottages are built of limestone rubble, usually with more regular gritstone quoins and window surrounds. Like the warm, brown gritstone town houses of the larger villages like Bakewell and Matlock, these older houses are often roofed in gritstone slabs, which have sometimes later been replaced by blue Welsh slate. Out in the country, the barns and farm buildings also reflect the available building stone, which is repeated in the endless miles of drystone walls of the Peak. In the former coalfield towns and villages of the east of the county, and in the clay vales to the south of Ashbourne, Midland red brick is the most common building material. In the larger industrial towns served by railways, such as Derby, Chesterfield, Belper and Ilkeston, blue engineering bricks are often employed on larger industrial buildings, and Victorian civic pride is reflected in grandiose town halls.

Derbyshire today is perhaps best known for the Peak District National Park, the first to be designated in Britain in 1951 in recognition of its outstanding scenery. It covers 555 square miles of the north of the county, taking in the limestone plateau and dales of the White Peak, and the brooding gritstone moors and edges of the Dark Peak. Over 22 million day visits are made to the National Park every year, making it the second most visited National Park in the world. But those visitors who only flock to the hills and dales of the Peak are missing a lot of what Derbyshire has to offer. It is indeed a county of contrasts, as we can see here in this second selection of Francis Frith's photographs, most of which were taken at the turn of the 19th century.

DERBYSHIRE REVISITED

ASHFORD IN THE WATER, *The Old Pump c1955* A324025

The pump at Ashford, on the left, is the site of one of the village's six well-dressings, held annually in early June. Note the milk lorry loaded with churns parked in Buxton Road, which leads off to the right.

▶ **ASHBOURNE**
The Church 1896
37873

Once famously described by the novelist George Eliot as 'the finest mere parish church in England', St Oswald's parish church at Ashbourne has long been regarded as one of Derbyshire's finest. It dates from the 13th century, and its soaring 212ft spire is a landmark for miles around.

◀ **ASHFORD IN THE WATER,** *The Mill c1955* A324004

Although described in this 1950s photograph as 'The Mill', this sturdy 18th-century cottage at picturesque Ashford in the Water, near Bakewell, looks more like a farmhouse, with its barn and stables on the left. Ashford was a centre of lead mining in the 18th and 19th centuries, and is now a popular tourist village.

ASHWOOD DALE, *Lover's Leap c1862* 1473

Lover's Leap in Ashwood Dale, near Buxton, is one of several in the Peak which recall a long-forgotten romantic tragedy. It is just visible in the depths of a limestone cleft to the south (left) of the main dale as you approach Buxton on what is now the A6.

▲ **ASHWOOD DALE** *c1876* 8822

Ashwood Dale is just one of the names given to the deep limestone valley of the River Wye as it winds between Bakewell and Buxton. Others include Monsal Dale, Miller's Dale and Chee Dale, and it only becomes Wye Dale and Ashwood Dale as it approaches Buxton.

▶ **BAKEWELL,** *The Church from the South-West 1890* 24627

This photograph, taken from the churchyard, shows the hilltop church of All Saints, Bakewell, as it appeared about 40 years after the major rebuilding which took place between 1841-52. The unusual octagonal tower topped by its elegant spire forms the backdrop to many views of the ancient market town and capital of the Peak.

▲ **BAKEWELL**
The Church, the Choir looking East 1890 24629

The most striking feature of this view of Bakewell church's choir and east end are the mass of brightly-coloured paintings which adorn the walls. After the major restoration of the chancel which took place shortly after this photograph was taken, all the walls were whitewashed, and remain so today.

◀ **BAKEWELL**
The Church, Dorothy Vernon's Tomb 1890 24630

The one tomb that every visitor wants to see in Bakewell church is that of Dorothy Vernon, who is alleged to have eloped from nearby Haddon Hall to marry local man John Manners. This is their joint tomb in the Vernon Chapel, erected after Sir John's death in 1584, and represents the couple's four children in its plinth.

BAKEWELL, *The View from Station Road 1914* 67613A

This is a classic view of the market town of Bakewell, seen from the steeply climbing Station Road. The spire of All Saints parish church on its hilltop site breaks the horizon, while to the right in the middle distance is the medieval bridge over the River Wye. Today, this scene would be dominated on the left by the futuristic shape of Bakewell's new Agricultural Business Centre.

▶ **BAKEWELL**
The Bridge 1923
73884

Bakewell Bridge has coped with ever-increasing traffic for six centuries, and remains one of the finest 14th-century town bridges in the country. The spire of the parish church is in the background of this peaceful summer view. Today, the banks of the Wye are usually thronged with tourists feeding the ducks in the river.

◀**BAKEWELL,** *Rutland Square c1955* B6011

The war memorial in the heart of Rutland Square is today surrounded by more extensive flowerbeds, but otherwise this scene from nearly half a century ago is little changed. The Red Lion public house and the National Westminster Bank in the centre of the picture are still there, but Burgon's grocery store (right) is long gone. However, older residents still refer to this as 'Burgon's Corner'.

▲ **BAMFORD,** *The Church 1919* 69176

Bamford's parish church of St John the Baptist is largely a William Butterfield restoration dating from 1861. It is probably most famous for the fact that the dead from the drowned village of Derwent were re-interred in its churchyard after the construction of the Ladybower Dam during the Second World War.

◀**BAMFORD**
1919 69177

This view of Bamford's Main Road is largely unchanged today - the rows of semi-detached villas still line the street as it climbs up towards the parish church, hidden in the trees to the right. In the background we can see the rocky gritstone escarpment of Bamford Edge.

▼ **BAMFORD,** *The Ladybower Dam and Win Hill c1955* B483006

This view looks across the ornate, wrought iron gates of the Ladybower Dam towards the newly planted regimented forestry on the slopes of Win Hill. The Ladybower Dam was constructed between 1935 and 1943; it was officially opened by King George VI at these gates on 25 September 1945, just 10 years before this photograph was taken.

▶ **BAMFORD**
*The Ladybower
Reservoir c1960*
B483020

We can just see the Ladybower Dam at the end of the reservoir in this view from the Snake Road. The noble escarpment in the left background is Bamford Edge. The Ladybower Reservoir, the last in the series of three which flooded the Upper Derwent Valley, was built to provide water for Sheffield and the East Midlands.

◀ **BAMFORD**
*The Howden Dam,
the Derwent
Valley c1965*
B483039

This fine view of the Howden Dam, with the forbidding moorland of Bleaklow beyond, is taken from Abbey Bank, on the edge of the Howden Moors. The Howden Dam was built between 1901 and 1912 and was the first in the series of three in the Derwent Valley to be completed.

▶ **BARLBOROUGH**
The Hall c1955 B803002

Sometimes described as the county's finest unspoilt Elizabethan country house, Barlborough Hall has stood to the north of Barlborough, a north-east Derbyshire village, for four centuries. The ornate, lantern-towered and mullioned structure was built for Lord Justice Francis Rodes to a design attributed to Robert Smythson in 1584, and remains in private hands.

▲ **BASLOW,** *The Bridge c1870* 5217

Riverside beeches frame Baslow's three-arched medieval bridge at Nether End, as it strides across the River Derwent with elegant ease. It is one of two bridges in the village - the other one at Bridge End dates from the 17th century, and features a tiny toll house with a 3½ ft (1m) high doorway.

▶ **BASLOW,** *Thatch End c1955*
B484020

These cottages at Thatch End, Baslow, standing near the bridge in photograph No 5217 above, are a Peak District rarity. Although heather thatching was once common in lowlier buildings, thatching was rarely used on substantial village cottages like these because the abundant local thin gritstone slates were preferred for roofing.

BERESFORD DALE *1919* 69175

This stone-walled lane leading down into Beresford Dale from the west is known as Beresford Lane. Beresford Dale is a northern extension of the more famous Dove Dale, and leads up towards the market village of Hartington.

BOLSOVER
The Castle 1902
48903

This view shows Sir Charles Cavendish's 17th-century 'Little Castle', or keep, at Bolsover Castle. Recently extensively renovated by its current custodians, English Heritage, Bolsover Castle was originally built high on a limestone crag overlooking the town by William Peveril, illegitimate son of William the Conqueror.

BOLSOVER, *The Castle 1902* 48907

The ivy-clad Western Terrace at Bolsover, built by Charles Cavendish's son, William, commands fine views over the valleys of the River Rother and Doe Lea. The roofless wing has been consolidated by English Heritage, but no longer sports the luxuriant growth of ivy we see here.

BONSALL, *Via Gellia, the Pig of Lead Inn 1892* 31300

Lead mining was still very much a local industry in Bonsall when this photograph was taken outside the Pig of Lead Inn. The people in the photograph are interesting, from the horse and cart and man carrying a basket and harness on the left, to the two boys, one dressed in a sailor suit, and a man who may be their father in a straw boater in the centre.

► **BONSALL**
Via Gellia, Tufa Cottage 1886
18586

Tufa Cottage, on the Via Gellia road from Cromford to Bonsall, was constructed entirely from blocks of tufa, the stone deposited by lime-rich water in this limestone country. A woman poses in her horse-drawn trap. The road was named after Phillip Gell of Cromford, who had it built in the late 18th century.

◄ **BRADWELL**
From the Bridge c1955
B486017

Bradwell is a bustling little former lead mining village on the south side of the Hope Valley in north Derbyshire. This view from the bridge over the Bradwell Brook looks north up the main village street, with the Bridge House Café and Pearce's ice cream shop on the right - Bradwell is famous for its home-made ice cream - and Bradwell's newsagent on the left.

▲ **BRETBY,** *The Hall c1955* B768301

Bretby Hall, or Bretby Park, which stands in its own 600-acre park near Burton on Trent, is a mock-Gothic, castellated pile built in 1813 by Sir Jeffrey Wyatville; it is now used as a hospital. The original house was built for the 2nd Earl of Chesterfield to a design by Inigo Jones.

◀**BRIMINGTON**
High Street c1965
B603016

Brimington is one of a number of similar former coal mining villages to the east of Chesterfield, and today villages like this are seeking a new identity. But coal was still king when this photograph was taken of the High Street, and the post office, on the left, was a centre of village activity.

BUXTON, *The Crescent 1896* 37851

This classic view of Buxton from The Slopes was taken during its heyday as an inland spa created largely by the efforts of the 5th Duke of Devonshire. In the centre is the magnificent 154ft diameter dome of the Great Stables and Riding School, at the time the largest unsupported dome in the world, while to the right in the background is the Palace Hotel. In the right foreground is Buxton's famous Crescent, recently renovated but still awaiting a new use, and to the left are the Natural Baths and the Old Hall Hotel.

BUXTON, *The Thermal Baths and the Crescent 1923* 74120

This view shows the end of the Crescent Hotel and the Thermal Baths (right), and was taken from Spring Gardens. Buxton's warm springs are thought to have been first discovered by the Romans, but it was the Duke of Devonshire who really popularised the lofty Georgian town (its stands at over 1,000ft above the sea), with developments like the Thermal Baths.

▼ **BUXTON,** *The Pavilion c1871* 5210

The beautiful cast iron tracery of the Pavilion was only completed in 1871, so it was brand new when this photograph was taken. Designed by Edward Milner of Sydenham, it was built to allow visitors who were taking the waters the space to relax indoors, sheltered from Buxton's notoriously cold weather.

▶ **BUXTON**
The Promenading Corridor, The Pavilion c1871 5211

Top-hatted gentlemen and crinoline-clad ladies promenade along the specially constructed corridor inside the Pavilion, shortly after its opening in 1871. Note the child wearing pantaloons holding her mother's hand in the middle distance.

◀ **BUXTON**
The Pavilion Gardens 1886
18657

Edward Milner was also responsible for the design of the 23 acres of gardens which adjoin the Pavilion at Buxton. This view looks towards the main entrance of the Pavilion, with ladies using their umbrellas to protect them against the rare summer sun.

▶ **BUXTON**
The Pavilion Gardens c1871 5201

The Serpentine Walks were carefully landscaped by Milner to give visitors to the spa a pleasant, relaxing experience after their treatment. Over a century later, the Pavilion Gardens still provide the nucleus of the town's leisure activities, with Frank Matcham's beautifully-restored Opera House close by.

► **BUXTON,** *Poole's Cavern Gardens c1862* 1461

Poole's Cavern has been a major tourist attraction ever since Mary Queen of Scots visited it during her incarceration here in the 16th century. Three centuries later, its landscaped gardens were studded with niches for classical statues and urns, as we can see in this rare, early photograph.

◄**CALVER**
Cliff College c1950
C399005

A view from the gardens of the imposing front of Cliff College at Calver, in the valley of the River Derwent, near Bakewell. This Methodist institution has a fine record for the training of ministers and teachers, and is now used for conferences and many other secular events.

▲ **CASTLETON,** *General View showing Mam Tor c1864* 2121

This early photograph of Castleton at the head of the Hope Valley shows the intricate network of drystone walls which surrounds the village. In the background (left) is the 'Shivering Mountain' of Mam Tor, so called because of the frequent landslips which occur on its east face. Beneath it is the old road to Chapel en le Frith, which is now closed to traffic.

◄ **CASTLETON**
Peveril Castle c1864
2123

Henry II's 12th-century keep at Castleton, seen here from Cave Dale with Lose Hill in the background, was an obvious sign of the Norman's dominance of the Peak District. Peveril Castle was originally built by William Peveril, illegitimate son of the Conqueror, to administer the Royal Hunting Forest of the Peak.

CASTLETON, *Peveril Castle 1896* 37837

A closer view of Henry II's keep at Peveril Castle. It was at Peveril where he accepted the submission of King Malcolm of Scotland in 1157, and he built this splendid stone keep 19 years later. It remains the finest medieval landmark in the Peak, and was formerly the symbol of the Peak District National Park.

CASTLETON
Cross Street 1932
85236

Cross Street is the main shopping street in Castleton, where gift shops still specialise in selling jewellery and other items made from the town's unique semi-precious stone, Blue John. By 1932, when this photograph was taken, tourism was already very important to the town, as we can see from the signs for tea shops and film.

CASTLETON, *The Memorial Cross 1919* 69167

Castleton's war memorial cross in the Market Place was still a relatively new feature when this photograph was taken. Taking the form of a Celtic cross, it remembered the dead of the town during the First World War, which had ended just a year before.

► **CASTLETON**
Goosehill Bridge
1909 61780

Goosehill Bridge crosses Peakshole Water, which emerges from the depths of Peak Cavern - its enclosing limestone cliffs can be seen in the background. The show cavern recently reverted to its robust ancient name of 'The Devil's Arse'.

◄ **CASTLETON**
Peak Cavern c1864
2126

A closer view of the massive entrance to Peak Cavern, said to be the largest cave entrance in Britain. Clearly visible are the wooden, gibbet-like frames used by the rope makers who made their home inside the cave entrance for hundreds of years. This was the famed 'village which never saw the sun'.

▲ **CASTLETON,** *Speedwell Cavern, The Landing Stage c1955* C46061

Speedwell Cavern, at the foot of the Winnats Pass, is another of Castleton's famous show caves. But this one has to be visited by boat, as it lies at the end of a half-mile underground canal originally excavated by lead miners. The canal is reached by a 104-step descent to this landing stage.

◀ **CASTLETON**
The Winnats Pass c1864
2130

A horse-drawn coach, led by a top-hatted coachman, negotiates the spectacular Winnats Pass, west of Castleton. This awesome cleft's name derives from Old English words meaning 'wind gates' - a reference to the howling winds which blow down this limestone ravine, which was created under a tropical sea 350 million years ago.

CASTLETON, *The Winnats Pass 1909* 61787

A flock of sheep pose obligingly for Francis Frith's photographer near the head of the Winnats Pass, near Castleton. This road was the ancient way into the town from the west from Chapel en le Frith, but plans to close it to traffic in the 1970s were thwarted when the alternative road under Mam Tor finally collapsed.

CHAPEL EN LE FRITH, *The Old Cross c1940* C400013

The Old Market Cross in Chapel en le Frith's Market Place is undated, but certainly medieval in origin. Chapel was established as a borough, entitled to hold markets and fairs, between 1220 and 1230, and the original parish church was built around 1225.

CHAPEL EN LE FRITH, *Market Place c1960* C400025

This is a general view of Chapel's cobbled market place, one of the highest in the county at 760ft above the sea. As we can see in this photograph, the market place stands above the main road through the town, and so is often missed by visitors. The tower of the parish church of St Thomas à Becket rises on the extreme left.

► **CHATSWORTH**
The House 1886 18643

This is the classic view of the Duke of Devonshire's mainly 17th-century Derbyshire home of Chatsworth, seen from James Paine's entrance bridge over the River Derwent. The only change that modern visitors to Derbyshire's most popular stately home will note are that the classical statues on the bridge piers are no longer present.

◀ **CHATSWORTH,**
*The House, View
showing the Italian
Gardens c1870* 5227

Here we see the east front of
Chatsworth, where a team of
gardeners with their carts full
of bedding plants are
working on the Italian
gardens. These gardeners
could well have been
employed by Joseph Paxton,
the great engineering genius
who joined the Duke of
Devonshire's staff in 1826.

▶ **CHATSWORTH**
The House, the French Gardens c1870 5228

At the time of this photograph, these were known as the French Gardens; they are now known as the Rose Garden. In the right background is the 1st Duke of Devonshire's early greenhouse, constructed in 1698.

◀ **CHATSWORTH**
The Palm House c1876 8849

This very rare photograph, taken around 1876, is captioned the Palm House, but it shows what was usually known as the Great Conservatory. Demolished shortly after the First World War, this magnificent structure was the brainchild of Joseph Paxton; at the time of its completion in 1840, it was the largest conservatory in the world. Using the experience he gained at Chatsworth, Paxton went on to design the Crystal Palace for the Great Exhibition in London in 1851.

CHATSWORTH
The Park, an Old Oak Tree c1864 2243

The old deer park at Chatsworth contains some of the oldest oak trees still living in Britain. These veteran trees, such as this one, can be up to 500 years old, and were once part of the medieval forest of Sherwood. Today, they are valued as important wildlife habitats for insects and fungi.

◀**CHEE DALE**
1914 67601

A view of the River Wye as it flows through the limestone gorge of Chee Dale, between Bakewell and Buxton. The limestone cliffs overhanging on the left of the photograph shade clumps of water-loving butterbur, the leaves of which were once used to keep butter cool and fresh.

CHESTERFIELD,
Midland Station 1896
37795A

This is a general view of Chesterfield, Derbyshire's second largest town, from the east. Prominent in the middle distance is the Midland Railway Company's station, recently completely re-built and modernised, and beyond that rise the tower of the Town Hall and the famous twisted spire of the parish church.

CHESTERFIELD
High Street 1896 37801

We are looking along Chesterfield's High Street from the cobbled Market Place - a scene little changed today. Horses and carts no longer park outside the Wheatsheaf public house, however; but the spire of the parish church can still be seen in the background at the end of Burlington Street, which like the High Street is now pedestrianised.

▲ **CHESTERFIELD,** *Market Place 1902* 48882

Another view of Chesterfield's sloping Market Place.
The Italianate, red brick Market Hall with its
imposing clock tower was built in 1857, and still
forms the centrepiece of the town's lively regular
outdoor market.

▶ **CHESTERFIELD,** *The Church 1902* 48888

Chesterfield's most famous icon is the twisted spire
of its parish church of St Mary and All Saints. The
twisting is thought to have been caused through the
use of unseasoned timbers when it was built at the
end of the 13th century. This view from the north
shows a group of Edwardian children gazing
quizzically at the camera.

▲ **DERBY,** *Iron Gate and the Cathedral c1955* D24011

The stately 212ft-high Perpendicular tower of Derby's Cathedral of All Saints, which dominates this view of Iron Gate, still exerts a powerful influence on the county's biggest city. The tower was built in the early years of the 16th century, but the rest of the building was completely rebuilt by James Gibbs between 1723-25.

◄ **DERBY,** *St Peter's Church c1960* D24062

This view of St Peter's Church, which stands at the junction of St Peter's Street and East Street in the city centre, shows just how busy the traffic was then. The woman with the pram has just successfully crossed the road at the junction, which is now much safer as the area is pedestrianised.

DOVEDALE, *The Stepping Stones 1914* 67611

Three women, all wearing ankle-length dresses, pose on Dovedale's famous Stepping Stones beneath the limestone crags of Thorpe Cloud (right). Dovedale is probably the best known of the Derbyshire Dales; indeed, the parked wagons offering donkey rides, and the signs to the Izaak Walton Hotel, show that tourism was already well-established when this photograph was taken.

DOVEDALE, *Ilam Rock 1894* 34260

Ivy-clad Ilam Rock rises dramatically from the banks of the River
Dove. The riverside path is clearly visible on the right, Derbyshire,
bank; today the bank is largely covered by trees, and the path
has had to be engineered to cope with the dale's huge number
of visitors.

DOVEDALE, *Reynard's Cave 1914* 67604

A family group prepare their picnic on the banks of the River Dove beneath the natural arch known as Reynard's Cave. This scene today would be largely obscured by trees, which have grown up since grazing ceased in the dale.

DOVEDALE, *Reynard's Cave from Above c1864* 2087

This view looks down on Reynard's Cave and the River Dove. The wooded slopes in the background are on the Staffordshire bank of the Dove, and rise to Air Cottage on the top of the hill opposite.

▼ **DOVEDALE,** *The Lion Rock 1899* 34261

The distinctive profile of the Lion Rock frowns down on the River Dove in the part of Dovedale known descriptively as the Narrows. This part of the path passes very close to the river, which is always liable to flooding, so a raised boardwalk has been constructed by the current owners, the National Trust, to assist walkers.

▶ **DRONFIELD,** *The War Memorial c1965*
D177048

A solitary soldier from the First World War stands sentinel on Dronfield's simple war memorial in the main street, opposite the White Swan public house (the licensee in 1965 was Alfred Edward Greeves). Dronfield lies midway between Chesterfield and Sheffield, and has developed as a commuter town for both.

◀ **ECKINGTON**
The Cross c1955
E226003

Eckington is another north-east Derbyshire town which formerly depended on the collieries which surrounded it, but which now is finding a new focus as a commuter town for Chesterfield and Sheffield. The Market Place and Cross, now partly pedestrianised, is situated just off the mile-long High Street.

▶ **EYAM,** *The Village 1896*
37811

The twin-gabled cottages in the centre of this photograph are where the infamous plague first struck in 1665. The story of the heroic, self-imposed quarantine which the villagers imposed to stop the infection spreading is well known. We can see the tower of the parish church of St Lawrence, where the minister, William Mompesson, led the sacrifice, in the left background.

▲ **EYAM,** *The Village 1919* 69208

The colonnaded porch on the left belongs to the Village Institute, a kind of working men's club, which originally catered for the many lead miners who lived in the village. It stands opposite the trees of the churchyard on the right of the photograph.

▶ **EYAM,** *The Saxon Cross 1896* 37815

The vigorously carved Saxon cross which stands in Eyam's churchyard is thought to date from around the 9th century, and is similar is style to the crosses at Bakewell. It was originally a preaching cross set out in the countryside. At some point it was damaged at the top of its shaft, and today it presents a somewhat truncated appearance.

▲ **EYAM,** *The Hall 1896* 37816

Eyam Hall, dating from the late 17th century, has been in the hands of the Wright family for over 300 years. Recently opened to the public for the first time, it gives a wonderfully intimate picture of a small country house. There are some fine tapestries in the upstairs rooms.

◀ **EYAM,** *The Hall and the Stocks 1919* 69210

What could be more English than the stocks (now restored) on the village green, with the manor house in the background? This scene has hardly changed in the three centuries since the house was built by the Wright family.

▶ **EYAM,** *Middleton Dale, Shining Cliff 1919* 69217

The massive limestone buttresses of Shining Cliff look down on the junction of Middleton Dale with the road to Eyam on the left of the photograph. The buildings on the junction in this photograph are no longer there, and the dale is now extensively quarried along its southern side.

◀ **EYAM,** *Middleton Dale, the View looking East 1896* 37823

This view of Middleton Dale, near Eyam, has totally changed today. The A623 Chesterfield-Chapel en le Frith road is now almost completely surrounded by tall trees, which obscure the limestone crags we can see in this picture.

▲ **FROGGATT,** *The Bridge 1896* 37807

The elegant double-span bridge over the River Derwent at Froggatt dates from the 17th century; it is unusual in that it has a large, pointed central arch nearer to the village and a smaller one on the other side. The smaller arch probably formed part of the original, smaller structure.

◄ **GOYT VALLEY**
General View 1894
34249

The gatehouse and gardeners' cottages on the approach to Errwood Hall at Goyt's Bridge in the Goyt Valley. All this lovely scene has now disappeared under the waters of the Errwood Reservoir, which was constructed in 1937.

GOYT VALLEY, *The Stepping Stones 1914* 67587

Two children, perhaps a brother and sister, negotiate the stepping stones across the infant River Goyt downstream from Goyt's Bridge in the peaceful days just before war broke out in Europe. Again, this scene disappeared under the rising waters of the Errwood Reservoir, and will never be seen again.

GREAT HUCKLOW,
The Village c1960
G180019

Great Hucklow is a former lead mining village high on the White Peak plateau of the Peak District. The main village street was deserted, apart from a small boy standing outside his house in the middle distance, when this photograph was taken.

GREAT LONGSTONE, *The Crispin Inn c1950* G181006

The name of the Crispin Inn in Great Longstone recalls one of the village's former specialities, boot and shoe making - St Crispin is the patron saint of that trade. Great Longstone's boots and shoes were made for the many local people who practiced a dual economy of farming and lead mining.

69

► **GRINDLEFORD,**
The View from
Goatscliff c1960
G182020

The Goatscliff entrance to the village of Grindleford is little changed today from the day when this photograph was taken. In the background are the wooded slopes of Froggatt and White Edge and the National Trust's Longshaw Estate.

◄ **GRINDLEFORD**
The Village c1960
G182032

Grindleford's war memorial (left) at the foot of Sir William Hill in the upper part of the village is based on the design of Eyam's Saxon preaching cross, and so it repeats the strange truncated appearance of its neighbour.

▲ **HADDON,** *The Hall 1886* 18627

Often described as 'the most romantic and complete medieval manor house in England', Haddon Hall, the Derbyshire home of the Dukes of Rutland, is seen here on its limestone bluff overlooking the River Wye, three miles south of Bakewell.

◄ **HADDON,** *The Hall, the Courtyard c1862* 1436

Time-worn steps lead up into the lower courtyard of Haddon Hall, instantly recognisable as the backdrop to countless feature films. The first Haddon was built by William Peveril, the same descendant of the Conqueror who built Peveril Castle at Castleton, but the present building mainly dates from the rebuilding by Sir Richard Vernon in the 14th and 15th centuries.

► **HADDON,**
The Hall, the
Garden Front
c1860 282

A top-hatted and frock-coated gentleman surveys the garden front of Haddon Hall. At this time, the Dukes of Rutland had virtually deserted the hall and removed themselves to their other estate at Belvoir Castle in Leicestershire. Restoration began with the 9th Duke at the beginning of the 20th century.

◄ **HADDON,** *The Hall,*
the Drawing Room
1902 48191

Now known as the Great Chamber, this magnificent partly oak-panelled room was originally part of the 14th-century house, but it was largely reconstructed by Sir Henry Vernon in about 1500. It still contains some of Haddon's finest French and Flemish tapestries, as it did in this photograph.

▲ **HADDON,** *The Hall, the State Bedroom 1902* 48192

The great state bed of Haddon was removed during the 9th Duke's restoration, and is now kept in the picture gallery at Belvoir Castle. The wonderful 16th-century plaster relief over the fireplace in the bedroom depicts Orpheus charming the beasts, and shows some naïve representations of exotic animals including an elephant and monkeys.

◄ **HADDON**
*The Hall, the Stables
c1870* 5237

A real coach party - that is, a party using a coach and horses - arrives at the stable block at Haddon Hall. The bowler-hatted gentlemen alight to face the climb up to the house. The stable block is now used as a restaurant and tea room, and the topiary of a Manners peacock and a Vernon boar's head in the garden at the front has now grown much larger.

▼ **HATHERSAGE,** *North Lees Hall 1902* 48924

The Tudor tower house of North Lees Hall was one of seven halls built by Robert Eyre for his sons, all allegedly within sight of one another. North Lees, beneath the moors of Stanage Edge, is thought to be the model used by Charlotte Bronte for Thornfield Hall in her novel *Jane Eyre.*

▶ **HATHERSAGE,** *Toad's Mouth Rock 1902* 48935

Someone carved an eye on this strange-shaped gritstone boulder to increase its resemblance to the warty amphibian. Toad's Mouth stands on the moors to the east of Hathersage near Burbage Bridge, where it overhangs the A625 Fox House road.

◄**HATHERSAGE**
*Leadmill Bridge
1896* 37806

The handsome Leadmill Bridge, on the Grindleford approach to Hathersage, spans the Derwent in three graceful gritstone arches. It takes its name from the hamlet of Leadmill, which in turn must have got its name from a former lead smelting site there.

► **HATHERSAGE,**
*The View from The
Station 1919* 69191

Mock Tudor villas were just beginning to spread out from the suburbs of Sheffield on to the former green fields of Hathersage when this photograph was taken. The Hope Valley railway line, in the middle distance, was opened in 1894, making the village even more attractive to commuters.

HATHERSAGE
The George 1919 69193

The George, a former
coaching inn, has stood at
the junction of the
Grindleford Road and the
Sheffield Road in
Hathersage for about 300
years. In this photograph,
an early automobile chugs
down the street, past a
white-coated delivery boy
pushing a handcart outside
the inn.

▼ **HATHERSAGE,** *Little John's Grave 1932* 85254

The legendary resting place of Robin Hood's loyal lieutenant has been pointed out to visitors to Hathersage churchyard for many years, and has been 'adopted' by the Ancient Order of Foresters, who look after it. Little John was said to be the son of a Hathersage nailor, and he died in a cottage (now demolished) to the east of the churchyard.

► **HAYFIELD**
The Packhorse Bridge c1960 H298008

The packhorse bridge over the Kinder River just outside Hayfield is also known locally as the Roman Bridge, but there is no evidence that Roman legionaries used it. It is much more likely to be a 17th- or 18th-century packhorse bridge, used by the 'jaggers' who carried goods by packhorse trains long before the days of metalled roads.

◄ **HAYFIELD**
Kinder Road c1960
H298012

Two ramblers enjoy the shade cast by the riverside trees as they walk towards Hayfield along the Kinder Road, which leads towards Kinder Scout. This was the route taken in 1932 by the ramblers on the infamous Kinder Scout Mass Trespass, after which five were imprisoned. The Mass Trespass, organised to deliberately publicise the situation where ramblers were excluded from large areas of mountain and moorland by a few grouse-shooting landlords, became an important catalyst for the National Parks and access to the countryside movement.

► **HAYFIELD,** *Kinder Scout from Kinder Road c1960* H298036

We are looking across the waters of the Kinder Reservoir. The drystone-walled fields lead up to the rocky heights of Kinder Scout, at 2,088ft the highest point in the Peak District. In the distance is Upper House Farm, one of many buildings around Kinder Scout which are now in the hands of the National Trust.

HOPE, *The Village*
1919 69180

Two white-collared Edwardian lads stand behind a trap outside the village smithy in the village which gave its name to the Hope Valley. Perhaps a sign of the times, an open-topped automobile is parked outside the Old Hall Hotel, opposite the tree-fringed churchyard.

HOPE, *The Village*
1932 85260

Another view of the Old Hall Hotel at Hope, this time taken from the raised bank of the churchyard. The Old Hall is on the site of the original manor house of the local Balguy family, from which it takes its name.

HOPE, *Green Lane 1919* 69183

A rustic seat adorns the entrance to this enticing green lane near the village of Hope. Many of these lanes are very ancient, lying on routes followed by packhorse trains and travellers over many hundreds of years, and now enjoyed by ramblers.

HOPE, *Moorgate and Lose Hill 1920* 69184

Lose Hill, at 1,563ft, is the eastern extremity of a fine ridge which runs from Mam Tor. It overlooks the village of Hope and the gabled house known as Moorgate (centre right), which now serves as a Countrywide (formerly Co-operative) Holidays Association guest house.

ILKESTON, *The Parish Church and the War Memorial c1955* I37036

The originally 14th-century pinnacled tower of St Mark's parish church watches over Ilkeston's wide Market Place, with the town's war memorial in the foreground. Double-decker buses wait to take their passengers to Derby and Kirk Hallam, and parking was yet to become a problem in the 1950s.

▶ **ILKESTON**
Bath Street c1949
I37039

Bath Street, leading off the Market Place, is one of Ilkeston's main shopping streets. This view looks back towards the tower of St Mark's at the end of the street. Again, traffic is notable by its absence, with only a single motor-cyclist to trouble crossing pedestrians.

◀ **ILKESTON**
High Street c1955
I37041

Another view of Bath Street, looking back towards the church. The range of shops is interesting, from Gunns the newsagents, selling the local *Nottingham Journal* and *Evening News* on the left, to the larger chain stores and building society offices.

◄ **LANGWITH**
High Street c1950
L295015E

There are actually two Langwiths - Nether and Upper - in north-east Derbyshire, near the border with Nottinghamshire and not far from Mansfield. Like so many other north-east Derbyshire communities, Langwith depended on coal for its livelihood, as we can see from the huge coal tip, now gone, visible in this view of the High Street.

LONG EATON, *Market Place c1950* L198014

This view of Long Eaton's Market Place is a real snapshot in time. The billiard rooms housed in the Oxford Buildings are on the right; the Palace Cinema is further down the street; and the cycle shop and the Rendezvous Milk Bar are opposite. All speak unmistakeably of the 1950s, when Frith's photographer called.

MAPLETON
Okeover Hall c1950
M348023

The Georgian red brick mansion of Okeover Hall (left) near Mapleton, north of Ashbourne, was built by the Okeover family in 1780, and shares a pleasant view across open parkland with the medieval church (centre). The village was depopulated in medieval times to make way for the Okeover's deer park.

MATLOCK, *The Bridge 1892* 31290

This sturdy gritstone bridge has spanned the mighty River Derwent in the centre of Derbyshire's county town for five centuries, although it has been widened and strengthened to take modern traffic. Intrepid canoeists can sometimes be seen negotiating the fast-flowing waters beneath.

MATLOCK, *The Queen's Head c1870* M273332

The Queen's Head Hotel, now shops, used to stand just across Matlock Bridge (from where this photograph was taken) on the way south towards Derby. The tall building in the distance to the right of The Queen's Head was then Matlock's post office.

MATLOCK, *The Square c1870* M273343

Now known as Crown Square, this busy junction at the centre of Matlock has always been the hub of the town. This view looks towards Matlock bridge, and tells of a time when local straw-hatted local people could stand in the middle of the street to have a leisurely conservation.

MATLOCK BANK
1892 31291

This view from the west shows John Smedley's massive Hydro on the opposite side of the valley, which brought spa town prosperity to the town after its erection in 1853. It stands at the top of the steep climb of Bank Road, in the centre of the picture. The Hydro buildings are now the offices of Derbyshire County Council.

► **MATLOCK BATH**
Derwent Terrace
c1864 2094

This view of Matlock Bath is taken from the station on the Midland line, and shows the beautiful setting of this Derwent-side village. Derwent Terrace, now the A6, runs alongside the river, faced by shops and with other houses spreading up the steep hillside.

◄ **MATLOCK BATH**
Derwent Terrace
1892 31277

This view of Derwent Terrace from the river shows the boathouses and boats which were used by visitors to this pleasant spa town. The spire of the parish church of Holy Trinity, built in 1842, punctuates the skyline.

▲ **MATLOCK BATH,** *The Promenade 1890* 24618

Another view of Derwent Terrace and the Promenade. This shows the Jubilee Bridge crossing the Derwent - the bridge was erected to mark the jubilee of Queen Victoria's reign.

◄ **MATLOCK BATH**
Lovers' Walk 1896 37877

The tree-lined walks by the side of the River Derwent known as the Lovers' Walks have been popular with visitors since the town became a tourist honeypot in the 19th century. They are still popular today, not least with the groups of leather-suited motor-cyclists who have made Matlock Bath their adopted weekend home.

95

▼ **MICKLEOVER,** *Uttoxeter Road c1950* M220030A

Mickleover, still known as 'the village' to its residents, is today not much more than a dormitory town to nearby Derby. But it still managed to retain something of that village atmosphere when this photograph was taken.

► **MILLER'S DALE**
c1862 1453

A top-hatted gentleman strides purposefully across the rickety wooden bridge across the River Wye in Miller's Dale in this charming view. Untouched by roads because of its precipitous limestone crags, Miller's Dale remains a sanctuary known only to walkers even today.

◄ **MONSAL DALE**
The View from the Bridge c1864 2146

A low, clapper-style footbridge across the River Wye in Monsal Dale leads to the hamlet of Upperdale, which we can see across the river. Beyond the scattered farms and cottages, the limestone hills sweep up towards the large exposed cutting, just visible above the trees to the right, which has been made for the imminent coming of the Midland Railway.

► **MONSAL DALE**
A Cottage c1864
2148

Surely everyone's dream of a Peak District cottage, this beautiful little building is situated between Monsal and Cressbrook Dales in the valley of the River Wye. The limestone rubble walls, the mullioned windows and the heather-thatched roof indicate that it probably dates from the 17th or 18th century.

MONSAL DALE, *The Viaduct c1955* M221015

The construction of the Midland line through the dales of the Wye excited the wrath of the early conservationist John Ruskin, and the Monsal Dale viaduct was thought to have particularly offended him. A freight train pulled by a steam locomotive is seen heading north across the viaduct towards Buxton.

MONSAL DALE
The Monsal Head Hotel c1955 M221004

The Monsal Head Hotel commands one of the finest and most photographed views in the Peak District, extending across the Monsal Dale Viaduct towards Fin Cop, and north towards Upperdale.

OLD WHITTINGTON, *The Revolution House 1902* 48902

The Revolution House, formerly the Cock and Pynot (or Magpie) Inn, at Old Whittington, north of Chesterfield, was the scene of the hatching of the plot for the Glorious Revolution of 1688, which aimed to place William of Orange on the English throne. The thatched cottage standing in front is now a museum.

▲ **PEAK DALE,** *Small Dale c1955*
P235012B

We are high on the limestone White Peak plateau with this photograph of farm buildings and cottages in the hamlet of Small Dale, north of Peak Dale, to the north east of Buxton. This whole area is now blighted by huge limestone quarries, including the one at Tunstead, which has one of the longest quarry faces in Europe.

▶ **PEAK DALE,** *Peak Forest Station c1955* P235012E

The station and extensive sidings at Peak Dale were mainly for the transportation of limestone from the surrounding quarries - we can see some of them in the background of this photograph. A steam locomotive waits at left centre.

REPTON,
The School c1955
R298016

Repton's famous public school was founded by Sir John Port of Etwall in 1556, but it was under the leadership of Dr Pears between 1854-74 that its fame and reputation really took off. This photograph shows the end of the Pears Memorial Hall, which was built on the foundations of the old priory church.

REPTON, *The Hall c1955* R298006

Here we see the headmaster's house at Repton, which is known as the Hall. It incorporates part of the 15th-century Prior Overton's Tower. Note the ornate, ball-topped entrance gate columns, and the earlier priory remains incorporated into the garden walls.

101

▼ **REPTON,** *Thatched Cottages c1955* R298028

These low, half-timbered and thatched cottages at Repton probably date from Tudor times; they give an indication of the antiquity of this sleepy township, which lies eight miles to the south-west of Derby.

ROWSLEY
The Peacock Inn c1864
2151

The mellow gritstone walls of the Peacock Hotel, on the A6 about four miles north of Matlock, are a landmark to visitors coming into the Peak District from the south. The inn dates from the mid 17th century; it was originally a manor house for the agent to the Manners family at nearby Haddon Hall as we can see from their peacock crest over the porch.

◄ ROWSLEY
*The Bridge and
the Peacock Inn
c1870* 5216

The bridge over the
River Derwent at
Rowsley was built in
the early 17th century,
and still carries
today's busy traffic on
the A6 trunk road. In
the background we
can see the chimneys
of the Peacock Inn,
which we see in
picture No 2151.

**► SOUTH
WINGFIELD**
The Church 1892
31304

South Wingfield's
parish church of All
Saints dates mainly
from the 13th century.
The style of its
crocketed spire and
castellated roof seems
to belong more to the
south Midlands than
to this pleasant village
two miles west of
Alfreton.

▼ **STRETTON,** *The Church c1960* S453016

Stretton - the name comes from the Old English, and refers to a settlement on a Roman road - is a small hamlet south of Clay Cross. True to its name, it is on the former Roman road which linked Derby and Chesterfield, and its solidly-built parish church looks like a miniature Liverpool Cathedral.

▶ **SWANWICK**
Derby Road c1955
S724009

The pinnacled tower of Swanwick's parish church stands four-square at the end of Derby Road. This small village (pronounced 'Swan'ick') lies on the A38, midway between Ripley and Alfreton, to the north of Derby.

◀ **TAXAL**
The Church c1955
T360009

Taxal is a small village south of Whaley Bridge, lying in a cul-de-sac overlooking the lovely Goyt Valley. Its mainly 19th-century parish church of St James, which we see here in its wooded setting, is in the diocese of Chester, recalling the fact that the village was in Cheshire until local government re-organisation transferred it to Derbyshire in 1936.

▶ **TAXAL**
Taxal Lodge School c1955 T360011

Taxal Lodge was a boarding school on the outskirts of the village. Note the single-storey extension and the fire escape ladder from the upper bedroom in the gable of the main building. The well-kept gardens made for a peaceful setting for the pupils.

▼ **TIDESWELL,** *The Church 1896* 37864

The magnificent parish church of St John the Baptist at Tideswell has justly earned the epithet 'the Cathedral of the Peak'. Built almost entirely in the Decorated style within 70 years from around 1300, it is one of the finest parish churches in the county, and a prominent local landmark.

► **TIDESWELL**
The Church, the Chancel 1896 37866

One of the greatest glories of Tideswell's parish church is its wonderfully light and airy chancel. This lightness is the result of the large, plain glass windows on either wall. In the foreground on the left are examples of the splendid wood carving which is such a feature in the church; it was executed by a local family, the Hunstones.

◄ **TIDESWELL**
The View from the Church Tower c1965 T46022

This view of Tideswell is from the pinnacled Perpendicular tower of the parish church. We are looking down on the Pot Market, where pots and pans were once bought and sold, and along Queen Street, the main shopping street of this small town on the White Peak plateau.

► **TIDESWELL**
Queen Street c1950 T46011

In the background (centre) is the Methodist chapel, a common feature of most former lead mining villages in the White Peak.

WHALEY BRIDGE, *The School 1898* 41135

Here we see pupils at play in the street outside the old school at Whaley Bridge. Note the pinafore-wearing girls and the white starched collars of the boys. In the background is the tower of the parish church.

▲ WHATSTANDWELL
Hillside c1960 W347024

This view looks down on the A6 trunk road, which passes across the centre of the picture, at Whatstandwell, seven miles west of Matlock. Between the trees in the foreground we can see a caravan park with what appears to be a dwelling made from a former railway carriage.

◄ WHATSTANDWELL
The River Derwent c1960 W347028

The bridge carries the A6 over the River Derwent in the background of this photograph, which was taken from the river. Whatstandwell gets its strange name from Walter Stonewell, a 14th-century resident, whose house was next to the former ford which crossed the river here.

WHITWELL, *The Square c1965* W349019

Whitwell stands at the entrance to the Duke of Portland's Welbeck Abbey, and it is in the heart of north-east Derbyshire's former coal mining country. This view of the village square, complete with its war memorial, shows the winding nature of the main village street; a coach is on its way to Chesterfield, 10 miles away to the west.

WHITWELL
The View from Sunnyside c1965
W349016

The chimneys, towers and winding wheels of the now-closed Whitwell Colliery dominate this view of the village. To the left we can see the village school with its walled playground.

WHITWELL, *The Old Hall c1965* W349011

The Old Hall, or Manor House, at Whitwell bears the mullioned and transomed windows and steep gables typical of its Tudor ancestry. The hall of the manor was once used as the hall for the village school. Note the fine oriel window on the first floor to the left.

111

▼ **WILLINGTON,** *The Green c1955* W557008

Willington stands on the Trent and Mersey Canal in the Trent valley to the south of Derby. This view shows a deserted village, with the branch of the Derby Co-operative Society (centre) waiting for its first customer of the day.

► **WILLINGTON**
The Willington Hotel c1955 W557012

Here we see the white-washed walls of the Willington Hotel. Willington is today overshadowed by the massive cooling towers of the huge power station to the east of the village.

◄ **WINSTER**
View of the Rocks
c1960 W569006

Winster Rocks, also known as Wyns Tor, are an outcrop of Dolomitic limestone to the south of the village, on what is now a long distance footpath known as the Limestone Way. The White Peak plateau rolls away in the distance.

► **WINSTER**
View from The Rocks
c1960 W569008

The village of Winster is one of the most complete 18th-century villages in Derbyshire, founded on the wealth won from the numerous lead mines which still pit the fields which surround it. The 17th-century Old Market Hall in the centre of the village was the first National Trust property in Derbyshire - the Trust acquired it in 1906.

▲ **WIRKSWORTH,** *The Market Place c1965* W351021

The steeply-sloping cobbled Market Place in the centre of Wirksworth was the centrepiece of the restoration of this former lead mining town, which won a Casa Nostra award in the 1980s. Wirksworth was the 'Snowfield' of George Eliot's novel *Adam Bede*.

► **YOULGREAVE,** *The River Bradford c1960* Y14011

The plateau-top village of Youlgreave stands between the valleys of the Bradford and the Lathkill; it is a prosperous settlement based on lead mining and farming. This view of the winding River Bradford below the village shows the limestone cliffs which line its reedy banks.

INDEX

Frith Book Co Titles

www.francisfrith.co.uk

The Frith Book Company publishes over 100 new titles each year. A selection of those currently available is listed below. For latest catalogue please contact Frith Book Co.
Town Books 96 pages, approximately 100 photos. **County and Themed Books** 128 pages, approximately 150 photos (unless specified). All titles hardback with laminated case and jacket, except those indicated pb (paperback)

Amersham, Chesham & Rickmansworth (pb)	1-85937-340-2	£9.99	Devon (pb)	1-85937-297-x	£9.99
Andover (pb)	1-85937-292-9	£9.99	Devon Churches (pb)	1-85937-250-3	£9.99
Aylesbury (pb)	1-85937-227-9	£9.99	Dorchester (pb)	1-85937-307-0	£9.99
Barnstaple (pb)	1-85937-300-3	£9.99	Dorset (pb)	1-85937-269-4	£9.99
Basildon Living Memories (pb)	1-85937-515-4	£9.99	Dorset Coast (pb)	1-85937-299-6	£9.99
Bath (pb)	1-85937-419-0	£9.99	Dorset Living Memories (pb)	1-85937-584-7	£9.99
Bedford (pb)	1-85937-205-8	£9.99	Down the Severn (pb)	1-85937-560-x	£9.99
Bedfordshire Living Memories	1-85937-513-8	£14.99	Down The Thames (pb)	1-85937-278-3	£9.99
Belfast (pb)	1-85937-303-8	£9.99	Down the Trent	1-85937-311-9	£14.99
Berkshire (pb)	1-85937-191-4	£9.99	East Anglia (pb)	1-85937-265-1	£9.99
Berkshire Churches	1-85937-170-1	£17.99	East Grinstead (pb)	1-85937-138-8	£9.99
Berkshire Living Memories	1-85937-332-1	£14.99	East London	1-85937-080-2	£14.99
Black Country	1-85937-497-2	£12.99	East Sussex (pb)	1-85937-606-1	£9.99
Blackpool (pb)	1-85937-393-3	£9.99	Eastbourne (pb)	1-85937-399-2	£9.99
Bognor Regis (pb)	1-85937-431-x	£9.99	Edinburgh (pb)	1-85937-193-0	£8.99
Bournemouth (pb)	1-85937-545-6	£9.99	England In The 1880s	1-85937-331-3	£17.99
Bradford (pb)	1-85937-204-x	£9.99	Essex - Second Selection	1-85937-456-5	£14.99
Bridgend (pb)	1-85937-386-0	£7.99	Essex (pb)	1-85937-270-8	£9.99
Bridgwater (pb)	1-85937-305-4	£9.99	Essex Coast	1-85937-342-9	£14.99
Bridport (pb)	1-85937-327-5	£9.99	Essex Living Memories	1-85937-490-5	£14.99
Brighton (pb)	1-85937-192-2	£8.99	Exeter	1-85937-539-1	£9.99
Bristol (pb)	1-85937-264-3	£9.99	Exmoor (pb)	1-85937-608-8	£9.99
British Life A Century Ago (pb)	1-85937-213-9	£9.99	Falmouth (pb)	1-85937-594-4	£9.99
Buckinghamshire (pb)	1-85937-200-7	£9.99	Folkestone (pb)	1-85937-124-8	£9.99
Camberley (pb)	1-85937-222-8	£9.99	Frome (pb)	1-85937-317-8	£9.99
Cambridge (pb)	1-85937-422-0	£9.99	Glamorgan	1-85937-488-3	£14.99
Cambridgeshire (pb)	1-85937-420-4	£9.99	Glasgow (pb)	1-85937-190-6	£9.99
Cambridgeshire Villages	1-85937-523-5	£14.99	Glastonbury (pb)	1-85937-338-0	£7.99
Canals And Waterways (pb)	1-85937-291-0	£9.99	Gloucester (pb)	1-85937-232-5	£9.99
Canterbury Cathedral (pb)	1-85937-179-5	£9.99	Gloucestershire (pb)	1-85937-561-8	£9.99
Cardiff (pb)	1-85937-093-4	£9.99	Great Yarmouth (pb)	1-85937-426-3	£9.99
Carmarthenshire (pb)	1-85937-604-5	£9.99	Greater Manchester (pb)	1-85937-266-x	£9.99
Chelmsford (pb)	1-85937-310-0	£9.99	Guildford (pb)	1-85937-410-7	£9.99
Cheltenham (pb)	1-85937-095-0	£9.99	Hampshire (pb)	1-85937-279-1	£9.99
Cheshire (pb)	1-85937-271-6	£9.99	Harrogate (pb)	1-85937-423-9	£9.99
Chester (pb)	1-85937-382 8	£9.99	Hastings and Bexhill (pb)	1-85937-131-0	£9.99
Chesterfield (pb)	1-85937-378-x	£9.99	Heart of Lancashire (pb)	1-85937-197-3	£9.99
Chichester (pb)	1-85937-228-7	£9.99	Helston (pb)	1-85937-214-7	£9.99
Churches of East Cornwall (pb)	1-85937-249-x	£9.99	Hereford (pb)	1-85937-175-2	£9.99
Churches of Hampshire (pb)	1-85937-207-4	£9.99	Herefordshire (pb)	1-85937-567-7	£9.99
Cinque Ports & Two Ancient Towns	1-85937-492-1	£14.99	Herefordshire Living Memories	1-85937-514-6	£14.99
Colchester (pb)	1-85937-188-4	£8.99	Hertfordshire (pb)	1-85937-247-3	£9.99
Cornwall (pb)	1-85937-229-5	£9.99	Horsham (pb)	1-85937-432-8	£9.99
Cornwall Living Memories	1-85937-248-1	£14.99	Humberside (pb)	1-85937-605-3	£9.99
Cotswolds (pb)	1-85937-230-9	£9.99	Hythe, Romney Marsh, Ashford (pb)	1-85937-256-2	£9.99
Cotswolds Living Memories	1-85937-255-4	£14.99	Ipswich (pb)	1-85937-424-7	£9.99
County Durham (pb)	1-85937-398-4	£9.99	Isle of Man (pb)	1-85937-268-6	£9.99
Croydon Living Memories (pb)	1-85937-162-0	£9.99	Isle of Wight (pb)	1-85937-429-8	£9.99
Cumbria (pb)	1-85937-621-5	£9.99	Isle of Wight Living Memories	1-85937-304-6	£14.99
Derby (pb)	1-85937-367-4	£9.99	Kent (pb)	1-85937-189-2	£9.99
Derbyshire (pb)	1-85937-196-5	£9.99	Kent Living Memories(pb)	1-85937-401-8	£9.99
Derbyshire Living Memories	1-85937-330-5	£14.99	Kings Lynn (pb)	1-85937-334-8	£9.99

Available from your local bookshop or from the publisher

Frith Book Co Titles (continued)

Title	ISBN	Price	Title	ISBN	Price
Lake District (pb)	1-85937-275-9	£9.99	Sherborne (pb)	1-85937-301-1	£9.99
Lancashire Living Memories	1-85937-335-6	£14.99	Shrewsbury (pb)	1-85937-325-9	£9.99
Lancaster, Morecambe, Heysham (pb)	1-85937-233-3	£9.99	Shropshire (pb)	1-85937-326-7	£9.99
Leeds (pb)	1-85937-202-3	£9.99	Shropshire Living Memories	1-85937-643-6	£14.99
Leicester (pb)	1-85937-381-x	£9.99	Somerset	1-85937-153-1	£14.99
Leicestershire & Rutland Living Memories	1-85937-500-6	£12.99	South Devon Coast	1-85937-107-8	£14.99
Leicestershire (pb)	1-85937-185-x	£9.99	South Devon Living Memories (pb)	1-85937-609-6	£9.99
Lighthouses	1-85937-257-0	£9.99	South East London (pb)	1-85937-263-5	£9.99
Lincoln (pb)	1-85937-380-1	£9.99	South Somerset	1-85937-318-6	£14.99
Lincolnshire (pb)	1-85937-433-6	£9.99	South Wales	1-85937-519-7	£14.99
Liverpool and Merseyside (pb)	1-85937-234-1	£9.99	Southampton (pb)	1-85937-427-1	£9.99
London (pb)	1-85937-183-3	£9.99	Southend (pb)	1-85937-313-5	£9.99
London Living Memories	1-85937-454-9	£14.99	Southport (pb)	1-85937-425-5	£9.99
Ludlow (pb)	1-85937-176-0	£9.99	St Albans (pb)	1-85937-341-0	£9.99
Luton (pb)	1-85937-235-x	£9.99	St Ives (pb)	1-85937-415-8	£9.99
Maidenhead (pb)	1-85937-339-9	£9.99	Stafford Living Memories (pb)	1-85937-503-0	£9.99
Maidstone (pb)	1-85937-391-7	£9.99	Staffordshire (pb)	1-85937-308-9	£9.99
Manchester (pb)	1-85937-198-1	£9.99	Stourbridge (pb)	1-85937-530-8	£9.99
Marlborough (pb)	1-85937-336-4	£9.99	Stratford upon Avon (pb)	1-85937-388-7	£9.99
Middlesex	1-85937-158-2	£14.99	Suffolk (pb)	1-85937-221-x	£9.99
Monmouthshire	1-85937-532-4	£14.99	Suffolk Coast (pb)	1-85937-610-x	£9.99
New Forest (pb)	1-85937-390-9	£9.99	Surrey (pb)	1-85937-240-6	£9.99
Newark (pb)	1-85937-366-6	£9.99	Surrey Living Memories	1-85937-328-3	£14.99
Newport, Wales (pb)	1-85937-258-9	£9.99	Sussex (pb)	1-85937-184-1	£9.99
Newquay (pb)	1-85937-421-2	£9.99	Sutton (pb)	1-85937-337-2	£9.99
Norfolk (pb)	1-85937-195-7	£9.99	Swansea (pb)	1-85937-167-1	£9.99
Norfolk Broads	1-85937-486-7	£14.99	Taunton (pb)	1-85937-314-3	£9.99
Norfolk Living Memories (pb)	1-85937-402-6	£9.99	Tees Valley & Cleveland (pb)	1-85937-623-1	£9.99
North Buckinghamshire	1-85937-626-6	£14.99	Teignmouth (pb)	1-85937-370-4	£7.99
North Devon Living Memories	1-85937-261-9	£14.99	Thanet (pb)	1-85937-116-7	£9.99
North Hertfordshire	1-85937-547-2	£14.99	Tiverton (pb)	1-85937-178-7	£9.99
North London (pb)	1-85937-403-4	£9.99	Torbay (pb)	1-85937-597-9	£9.99
North Somerset	1-85937-302-x	£14.99	Truro (pb)	1-85937-598-7	£9.99
North Wales (pb)	1-85937-298-8	£9.99	Victorian & Edwardian Dorset	1-85937-254-6	£14.99
North Yorkshire (pb)	1-85937-236-8	£9.99	Victorian & Edwardian Kent (pb)	1-85937-624-X	£9.99
Northamptonshire Living Memories	1-85937-529-4	£14.99	Victorian & Edwardian Maritime Album (pb)	1-85937-622-3	£9.99
Northamptonshire	1-85937-150-7	£14.99	Victorian and Edwardian Sussex (pb)	1-85937-625-8	£9.99
Northumberland Tyne & Wear (pb)	1-85937-281-3	£9.99	Villages of Devon (pb)	1-85937-293-7	£9.99
Northumberland	1-85937-522-7	£14.99	Villages of Kent (pb)	1-85937-294-5	£9.99
Norwich (pb)	1-85937-194-9	£8.99	Villages of Sussex (pb)	1-85937-295-3	£9.99
Nottingham (pb)	1-85937-324-0	£9.99	Warrington (pb)	1-85937-507-3	£9.99
Nottinghamshire (pb)	1-85937-187-6	£9.99	Warwick (pb)	1-85937-518-9	£9.99
Oxford (pb)	1-85937-411-5	£9.99	Warwickshire (pb)	1-85937-203-1	£9.99
Oxfordshire (pb)	1-85937-430-1	£9.99	Welsh Castles (pb)	1-85937-322-4	£9.99
Oxfordshire Living Memories	1-85937-525-1	£14.99	West Midlands (pb)	1-85937-289-9	£9.99
Paignton (pb)	1-85937-374-7	£7.99	West Sussex (pb)	1-85937-607-x	£9.99
Peak District (pb)	1-85937-280-5	£9.99	West Yorkshire (pb)	1-85937-201-5	£9.99
Pembrokeshire	1-85937-262-7	£14.99	Weston Super Mare (pb)	1-85937-306-2	£9.99
Penzance (pb)	1-85937-595-2	£9.99	Weymouth (pb)	1-85937-209-0	£9.99
Peterborough (pb)	1-85937-219-8	£9.99	Wiltshire (pb)	1-85937-277-5	£9.99
Picturesque Harbours	1-85937-208-2	£14.99	Wiltshire Churches (pb)	1-85937-171-x	£9.99
Piers	1-85937-237-6	£17.99	Wiltshire Living Memories (pb)	1-85937-396-8	£9.99
Plymouth (pb)	1-85937-389-5	£9.99	Winchester (pb)	1-85937-428-x	£9.99
Poole & Sandbanks (pb)	1-85937-251-1	£9.99	Windsor (pb)	1-85937-333-x	£9.99
Preston (pb)	1-85937-212-0	£9.99	Wokingham & Bracknell (pb)	1-85937-329-1	£9.99
Reading (pb)	1-85937-238-4	£9.99	Woodbridge (pb)	1-85937-498-0	£9.99
Redhill to Reigate (pb)	1-85937-596-0	£9.99	Worcester (pb)	1-85937-165-5	£9.99
Ringwood (pb)	1-85937-384-4	£7.99	Worcestershire Living Memories	1-85937-489-1	£14.99
Romford (pb)	1-85937-319-4	£9.99	Worcestershire	1-85937-152-3	£14.99
Royal Tunbridge Wells (pb)	1-85937-504-9	£9.99	York (pb)	1-85937-199-x	£9.99
Salisbury (pb)	1-85937-239-2	£9.99	Yorkshire (pb)	1-85937-186-8	£9.99
Scarborough (pb)	1-85937-379-8	£9.99	Yorkshire Coastal Memories	1-85937-506-5	£14.99
Sevenoaks and Tonbridge (pb)	1-85937-392-5	£9.99	Yorkshire Dales	1-85937-502-2	£14.99
Sheffield & South Yorks (pb)	1-85937-267-8	£9.99	Yorkshire Living Memories (pb)	1-85937-397-6	£9.99

See Frith books on the internet at www.francisfrith.co.uk

FRITH PRODUCTS & SERVICES

Francis Frith would doubtless be pleased to know that the pioneering publishing venture he started in 1860 still continues today. Over a hundred and forty years later, The Francis Frith Collection continues in the same innovative tradition and is now one of the foremost publishers of vintage photographs in the world. Some of the current activities include:

Interior Decoration

Today Frith's photographs can be seen framed and as giant wall murals in thousands of pubs, restaurants, hotels, banks, retail stores and other public buildings throughout the country. In every case they enhance the unique local atmosphere of the places they depict and provide reminders of gentler days in an increasingly busy and frenetic world.

Product Promotions

Frith products are used by many major companies to promote the sales of their own products or to reinforce their own history and heritage. Frith promotions have been used by Hovis bread, Courage beers, Scots Porage Oats, Colman's mustard, Cadbury's foods, Mellow Birds coffee, Dunhill pipe tobacco, Guinness, and Bulmer's Cider.

Genealogy and Family History

As the interest in family history and roots grows world-wide, more and more people are turning to Frith's photographs of Great Britain for images of the towns, villages and streets where their ancestors lived; and, of course, photographs of the churches and chapels where their ancestors were christened, married and buried are an essential part of every genealogy tree and family album.

Frith Products

All Frith photographs are available Framed or just as Mounted Prints and Posters (size 23 x 16 inches). These may be ordered from the address below. From time to time other products - Address Books, Calendars, Table Mats, etc - are available.

The Internet

Already fifty thousand Frith photographs can be viewed and purchased on the internet through the Frith websites and a myriad of partner sites.

For more detailed information on Frith companies and products, look at these sites:

www.francisfrith.co.uk
www.francisfrith.com
(for North American visitors)

See the complete list of Frith Books at:

www.francisfrith.co.uk

This web site is regularly updated with the latest list of publications from the Frith Book Company. If you wish to buy books relating to another part of the country that your local bookshop does not stock, you may purchase on-line.

For further information, trade, or author enquiries please contact us at the address below:
The Francis Frith Collection, Frith's Barn, Teffont, Salisbury, Wiltshire, England SP3 5QP.
Tel: +44 (0)1722 716 376 Fax: +44 (0)1722 716 881 Email: sales@francisfrith.co.uk

See Frith books on the internet at www.francisfrith.co.uk

FREE PRINT OF YOUR CHOICE

Mounted Print
Overall size 14 x 11 inches (355 x 280mm)

Choose any Frith photograph in this book.
Simply complete the Voucher opposite and return it with your remittance for £2.25 (to cover postage and handling) and we will print the photograph of your choice in SEPIA (size 11 x 8 inches) and supply it in a cream mount with a burgundy rule line (overall size 14 x 11 inches).
Please note: photographs with a reference number starting with a "Z" are not Frith photographs and cannot be supplied under this offer.
Offer valid for delivery to one UK address only.

PLUS: **Order additional Mounted Prints at HALF PRICE - £7.49 each** (normally £14.99)
If you would like to order more Frith prints from this book, possibly as gifts for friends and family, you can buy them at half price (with no additional postage and handling costs).

PLUS: **Have your Mounted Prints framed**
For an extra £14.95 per print you can have your mounted print(s) framed in an elegant polished wood and gilt moulding, overall size 16 x 13 inches (no additional postage and handling required).

IMPORTANT!

These special prices are only available if you use this form to order . You must use the ORIGINAL VOUCHER on this page (no copies permitted). We can only despatch to one UK address. This offer cannot be combined with any other offer.

Send completed Voucher form to:
The Francis Frith Collection, Frith's Barn, Teffont, Salisbury, Wiltshire SP3 5QP

CHOOSE A PHOTOGRAPH FROM THIS BOOK

Voucher for **FREE** and Reduced Price Frith Prints

Please do not photocopy this voucher. Only the original is valid, so please fill it in, cut it out and return it to us with your order.

Picture ref no	Page no	Qty	Mounted @ £7.49	Framed + £14.95	Total Cost £
		1	Free of charge*	£	£
			£7.49	£	£
			£7.49	£	£
			£7.49	£	£
			£7.49	£	£
			£7.49	£	£

Please allow 28 days for delivery.
Offer available to one UK address only

* Post & handling	£2.25
Total Order Cost	£

Title of this book . . . .

I enclose a cheque/postal order for £ . . . .
made payable to 'The Francis Frith Collection'

OR please debit my Mastercard / Visa / Maestro / Amex card, details below

Card Number

Issue No (Maestro only)   Valid from (Maestro)

Expires   Signature

Name Mr/Mrs/Ms . . . .
Address . . . .
. . . .
. . . .
. . . . Postcode . . . .
Daytime Tel No . . . .
Email . . . .

Valid to 31/12/07

Would you like to find out more about Francis Frith?

We have recently recruited some entertaining speakers who are happy to visit local groups, clubs and societies to give an illustrated talk documenting Frith's travels and photographs. If you are a member of such a group and are interested in hosting a presentation, we would love to hear from you.

Our speakers bring with them a small selection of our local town and county books, together with sample prints. They are happy to take orders. A small proportion of the order value is donated to the group who have hosted the presentation. The talks are therefore an excellent way of fundraising for small groups and societies.

Can you help us with information about any of the Frith photographs in this book?

We are gradually compiling an historical record for each of the photographs in the Frith archive. It is always fascinating to find out the names of the people shown in the pictures, as well as insights into the shops, buildings and other features depicted.

If you recognize anyone in the photographs in this book, or if you have information not already included in the author's caption, do let us know. We would love to hear from you, and will try to publish it in future books or articles.

Our production team

Frith books are produced by a small dedicated team at offices in the converted Grade II listed 18th-century barn at Teffont near Salisbury, illustrated above. Most have worked with the Frith Collection for many years. All have in common one quality: they have a passion for the Frith Collection. The team is constantly expanding, but currently includes:

Paul Baron, Phillip Brennan, Jason Buck, John Buck, Ruth Butler, Heather Crisp, David Davies, Louis du Mont, Isobel Hall, Gareth Harris, Lucy Hart, Julian Hight, Peter Horne, James Kinnear, Karen Kinnear, Tina Leary, Stuart Login, David Marsh, Lesley-Ann Millard, Sue Molloy, Glenda Morgan, Wayne Morgan, Sarah Roberts, Kate Rotondetto, Dean Scource, Eliza Sackett, Terence Sackett, Sandra Sampson, Adrian Sanders, Sandra Sanger, Jan Scrivens, Julia Skinner, David Smith, Miles Smith, Lewis Taylor, Shelley Tolcher, Lorraine Tuck, Amanita Wainwright and Ricky Williams.